May you continue to grow in your walk with Christ.

Jeremiah 29:11-13
Philippians 4:13

Stephanie Alloway

Julie Alloway

June 7, 1998

A QUIET PLACE

RESTING IN
GOD'S CARE

A Quiet Place: Resting in God's Care

A
QUIET
PLACE

RESTING IN
GOD'S CARE

The Message is a contemporary rendering of the Bible from
the original languages, crafted to present its tone, rhythm,
events, and ideas in everyday speech.

COME
AND REST

*J*esus resumed talking to the people,
but now tenderly....
"Are you tired? Worn out? Burned out on
religion? Come to me. Get away with me and
you'll recover your life. I'll show you how to
take a real rest. Walk with me and work with
me—watch how I do it. Learn the unforced
rhythms of grace. I won't lay anything heavy
or ill-fitting on you. Keep company with me
and you'll learn to live freely and lightly."

■ ■ ■ ■ ■ ■ ■ ■ ■ ■ ■ ■ ■

Matthew 11:27-30

R E S T

Come to Jesus, who presents us with a new
covenant, a fresh charter from God...
a proclamation of grace.

■ ■ ■ ■ ■ ■ ■ ■ ■ ■ ■ ■ ■ ■

Hebrews 12:24

REST

We look at this Son and see the God who cannot be seen. We look at this Son and see God's original purpose in everything created. For everything, absolutely everything, above and below, visible and invisible, rank after rank after rank of angels—everything got started in him and finds its purpose in him. He was there before any of it came into existence and holds it all together right up to this moment....

REST

He was supreme in the beginning and...
he is supreme in the end. From beginning to
end he's there, towering far above everything,
everyone. So spacious is he, so roomy, that
everything of God finds its proper place in him
without crowding. Not only that, but all the
broken and dislocated pieces of the universe—
people and things, animals and atoms—get
properly fixed and fit together in vibrant
harmonies, all because of his death.

■ ■ ■ ■ ■ ■ ■ ■ ■ ■ ■ ■ ■

Colossians 1:15-20

REST

*G*od does not respond to what *we* do; we respond to what *God* does. We've finally figured it out. Our lives get in step with God and all others by letting him set the pace, not by proudly or anxiously trying to run the parade....

REST

$\mathcal{B}$ut by shifting our focus from what *we* do to what *God* does, don't we cancel out all our careful keeping of the rules and ways God commanded? Not at all. What happens, in fact, is that by putting that entire way of life in its proper place, we confirm it.

■ ■ ■ ■ ■ ■ ■ ■ ■ ■ ■ ■ ■

Romans 3:27-28,31

REST

The promise of "arrival" and "rest" is still there for God's people. God himself is at rest. And at the end of the journey we'll surely rest with God.

■ ■ ■ ■ ■ ■ ■ ■ ■ ■ ■ ■ ■ ■

Hebrews 4:9-11

For as long, then, as that promise of resting in him pulls us on to God's goal for us, we need to be careful that we're not disqualified.... If we believe, though, we'll experience that state of resting.

■ ■ ■ ■ ■ ■ ■ ■ ■ ■ ■ ■ ■ ■

Hebrews 4:1,3

REST

Embrace this God-life. Really embrace
it, and nothing will be too much for you....
That's why I urge you to pray for absolutely
everything, ranging from small to large. Include
everything as you embrace this God-life,
and you'll get God's everything.

■ ■ ■ ■ ■ ■ ■ ■ ■ ■ ■ ■ ■

Mark 11:22-24

REST

$\mathscr{I}$t's useless to rise early and go to bed late,
and work your worried fingers to the bone.
Don't you know he enjoys
giving rest to those he loves?

■ ■ ■ ■ ■ ■ ■ ■ ■ ■ ■ ■ ■ ■

Psalm 127:2

REST

REST

$\mathcal{I}$'m an open book to you;
even from a distance, you know
what I'm thinking.
You know when I leave and when I get back;
I'm never out of your sight.

REST

You know everything I'm going to say
before I start the first sentence.
I look behind me and you're there,
then up ahead and you're there, too—
your reassuring presence, coming and going.

REST

This is too much, too wonderful—
I can't take it all in!
Is there anyplace I can go to avoid your Spirit?
to be out of your sight?
If I climb to the sky, you're there!
If I go underground, you're there!

REST

If I flew on morning's wings
to the far western horizon,
You'd find me in a minute—
you're already there waiting!

■ ■ ■ ■ ■ ■ ■ ■ ■ ■ ■ ■ ■ ■

Psalm 139:2-10

REST

"*If* you'll hold on to me for dear life,"
says GOD,
"I'll get you out of any trouble.
I'll give you the best of care
if you'll only get to know and trust me."

■ ■ ■ ■ ■ ■ ■ ■ ■ ■ ■ ■ ■ ■

Psalm 91:14

REST

$\mathscr{I}$s anyone thirsty? Come!
All who will, come and drink,
Drink freely of the Water of Life!

■ ■ ■ ■ ■ ■ ■ ■ ■ ■ ■ ■ ■

Revelation 22:17

REST

A PLACE
OF QUIET
RETREAT

You're my place of quiet retreat;
I wait for your Word to renew me....
I lovingly embrace everything you say.

■ ■ ■ ■ ■ ■ ■ ■ ■ ■ ■ ■ ■ ■

Psalm 119:114,119

REST

$\mathcal{Q}$uiet down before GOD,
be prayerful before him....
Wait passionately for GOD,
don't leave the path.
He'll give you your place in the sun.

■ ■ ■ ■ ■ ■ ■ ■ ■ ■ ■ ■ ■

Psalm 37:7,34

REST

His huge outstretched arms protect you—
under them you're perfectly safe;
his arms fend off all harm....
You'll stand untouched, watch it all
from a distance....
Yes, because GOD's your refuge,
the High God your very own home,

REST

Evil can't get close to you,
harm can't get through the door.
He ordered his angels
to guard you wherever you go.
If you stumble, they'll catch you;
their job is to keep you from falling.

■ ■ ■ ■ ■ ■ ■ ■ ■ ■ ■ ■ ■

Psalm 91:4-12

REST

$\mathcal{L}$ight, space, zest—
that's GOD!
So, with him on my side I'm fearless,
afraid of no one and nothing....
When besieged,
I'm calm as a baby.
When all hell breaks loose,
I'm collected and cool.

REST

I'm asking GOD for one thing,
only one thing:
To live with him in his house
my whole life long.
I'll contemplate his beauty;
I'll study at his feet.
That's the only quiet, secure place
in a noisy world.

■ ■ ■ ■ ■ ■ ■ ■ ■ ■ ■ ■ ■ ■

Psalm 27:1,3-5

REST

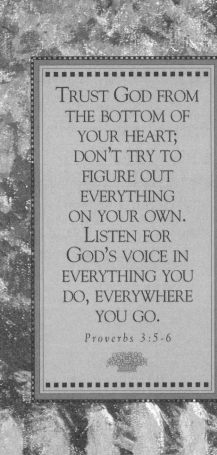

TRUST GOD FROM
THE BOTTOM OF
YOUR HEART;
DON'T TRY TO
FIGURE OUT
EVERYTHING
ON YOUR OWN.
LISTEN FOR
GOD'S VOICE IN
EVERYTHING YOU
DO, EVERYWHERE
YOU GO.

Proverbs 3:5-6

$\mathcal{G}$od is a safe place to hide,
ready to help when we need him.
We stand fearless at the cliff-edge of doom,
courageous in seastorm and earthquake,
Before the rush and roar of oceans,
the tremors that shift mountains....

REST

God fights for us.

■ ■ ■ ■ ■ ■ ■ ■ ■ ■ ■ ■ ■

Psalm 46:1-3

REST

*Y*ou've always given me breathing room,
a place to get away from it all,
A lifetime pass to your safe-house,
an open invitation as your guest.
You've always taken me seriously, God,
made me welcome.

■ ■ ■ ■ ■ ■ ■ ■ ■ ■ ■ ■ ■ ■

Psalm 61:3-5;62:1-2

REST

$\mathcal{G}$OD's a...sanctuary during bad times.
The moment you arrive, you relax.

■ ■ ■ ■ ■ ■ ■ ■ ■ ■ ■ ■ ■ ■

Psalm 9:9-10

$\mathcal{G}$OD became my hideout,
God was my high mountain retreat.

■ ■ ■ ■ ■ ■ ■ ■ ■ ■ ■ ■ ■ ■

Psalm 94:22

REST

God, the one and only—
I'll wait as long as he says.
Everything I hope for comes from him....
He's solid rock under my feet,
breathing room for my soul....

REST

So trust him absolutely, people;
lay your lives on the line for him.
God is a safe place to be.

■ ■ ■ ■ ■ ■ ■ ■ ■ ■ ■ ■ ■ ■

Psalm 62:5-6,8

REST

$\mathcal{I}$'m still in your presence,
but you've taken my hand.
You wisely and tenderly lead me,
and then you bless me.

REST

You're all I want in heaven!
You're all I want on earth!...
I'm in the very presence of God—
oh, how refreshing it is!
I've made Lord God my home.

■ ■ ■ ■ ■ ■ ■ ■ ■ ■ ■ ■ ■ ■ ■

Psalm 73:23-28

REST

CAREFREE
IN THE
CARE OF
GOD

If you decide for God, living a life of God-worship, it follows that you don't fuss about what's on the table at mealtimes or whether the clothes in your closet are in fashion. There is far more to your life than the food you put in your stomach, more to your outer appearance than the clothes you hang on your body. Look at the birds, free and unfettered, not tied down to a job description, careless in the care of God. And you count far more to him than birds.

REST

Has anyone by fussing in front of the mirror ever gotten taller by so much as an inch? All this time and money wasted on fashion—do you think it makes that much difference? Instead of looking at the fashions, walk out into the fields and look at the wildflowers. They never primp or shop, but have you ever seen color and design quite like it? The ten best-dressed men and women in the country look shabby alongside them.

REST

If God gives such attention to the appearance of wildflowers—most of which are never even seen—don't you think he'll attend to you, take pride in you, do his best for you? What I'm trying to do here is to get you to relax, to not be so preoccupied with getting, so you can respond to God's giving. People who don't know God and the way he works fuss over these things, but you know both God and how he works.

REST

Steep your life in God-reality, God-initiative, God-provisions. Don't worry about missing out. You'll find all your everyday human concerns will be met.

Give your entire attention to what God is doing right now, and don't get worked up about what may or may not happen tomorrow. God will help you deal with whatever hard things come up when the time comes.

■ ■ ■ ■ ■ ■ ■ ■ ■ ■ ■ ■ ■

Matthew 6:25-34

REST

*L*ive carefree before God;
he is most careful with you.

■ ■ ■ ■ ■ ■ ■ ■ ■ ■ ■ ■ ■ ■

1 Peter 5:7

*W*here you are right now is God's
place for you. Live and obey and love
and believe right there.

■ ■ ■ ■ ■ ■ ■ ■ ■ ■ ■ ■ ■ ■

1 Corinthians 7:17

REST

$\mathcal{A}$ cheerful heart brings a smile
to your face;
a sad heart makes it hard to get
through the day....
A cheerful disposition is good for your health.

■ ■ ■ ■ ■ ■ ■ ■ ■ ■ ■ ■ ■ ■

Proverbs 15:13;17:22

REST

Don't fret or worry. Instead of worrying, pray. Let petitions and praises shape your worries into prayers, letting God know your concerns. Before you know it, a sense of God's wholeness, everything coming together for good, will come and settle you down. It's wonderful what happens when Christ displaces worry at the center of your life....

REST

You'll do best by filling your minds and
meditating on things true, noble, reputable,
authentic, compelling, gracious—the best,
not the worst; the beautiful, not the ugly;
things to praise, not things to curse.... Do
that, and God, who makes everything
work together, will work you into
his most excellent harmonies.

■ ■ ■ ■ ■ ■ ■ ■ ■ ■ ■ ■ ■ ■

Philippians 4:6-9

REST

$\mathcal{I}$'ve learned by now to be quite content whatever my circumstances. I'm just as happy with little as with much, with much as with little. I've found the recipe for being happy whether full or hungry, hands full or hands empty. Whatever I have, wherever I am, I can make it through anything in the One who makes me who I am.

Philippians 4:11-13

REST

REST

$\mathscr{Y}$ou're blessed when you're content with just who you are—no more, no less. That's the moment you find yourselves proud owners of everything that can't be bought.

■ ■ ■ ■ ■ ■ ■ ■ ■ ■ ■ ■ ■

Matthew 5:5

REST

A devout life does bring wealth, but it's the rich simplicity of being yourself before God.

■ ■ ■ ■ ■ ■ ■ ■ ■ ■ ■ ■ ■ ■

1 Timothy 6:6

REST

$\mathcal{D}$o you want to stand out? Then step down. Be a servant. If you puff yourself up, you'll get the wind knocked out of you. But if you're content to simply be yourself, your life will count for plenty.

■ ■ ■ ■ ■ ■ ■ ■ ■ ■ ■ ■ ■ ■

Matthew 23:11-12

REST

$\mathcal{G}$OD takes care of all who stay close to him.

■ ■ ■ ■ ■ ■ ■ ■ ■ ■ ■ ■ ■ ■

Psalm 31:23

REST

There has never been the slightest doubt
in my mind that the God who started this
great work in you would keep at it and
bring it to a flourishing finish on the
very day Christ Jesus appears.

■ ■ ■ ■ ■ ■ ■ ■ ■ ■ ■ ■ ■ ■

Philippians 1:6

REST

May God himself, the God who makes everything holy and whole, make you holy and whole, put you together—spirit, soul, and body—and keep you fit for the coming of our Master, Jesus Christ. The One who called you is completely dependable. If he said it, he'll do it!

■ ■ ▨ ■ ■ ▨ ■ ■ ▨ ■ ■ ▨ ■

1 Thessalonians 5:23-24

REST

A
TAPESTRY
OF LOVE

I want you woven into a tapestry of love,
in touch with everything there is to know of
God. Then you will have minds confident and
at rest, focused on Christ, God's great mystery.
All the richest treasures of wisdom and
knowledge are embedded in that
mystery and nowhere else.

■ ■ ■ ■ ■ ■ ■ ■ ■ ■ ■ ■ ■ ■

Colossians 2:2-3

REST

$\mathcal{L}$ove...trusts God always.

■ ■ ■ ■ ■ ■ ■ ■ ■ ■ ■ ■ ■

1 Corinthians 13:4,7

REST

*I*mmense in mercy and with an incredible love, [God] embraced us. He took our sin-dead lives and made us alive in Christ. He did all this on his own, with no help from us! Then he picked us up and set us down in highest heaven in company with Jesus, our Messiah.

REST

Now God has us where he wants us, with all the time in this world and the next to shower grace and kindness upon us in Christ Jesus. Saving is all his idea, and all his work. All we do is trust him enough to let him do it. It's God's gift from start to finish!

■ ■ ■ ■ ■ ■ ■ ■ ■ ■ ■ ■ ■ ■

Ephesians 2:4-8

REST

$\mathcal{M}$ay the Master take you by the hand and
lead you along the path of God's love
and Christ's endurance.

■ ■ ■ ■ ■ ■ ■ ■ ■ ■ ■ ■ ■ ■

2 Thessalonians 3:4-5

REST

$\mathcal{I}$f you wake me each morning with the
sound of your loving voice,
I'll go to sleep each night trusting in you.
Point out the road I must travel;
I'm all ears, all eyes before you.

■ ■ ■ ■ ■ ■ ■ ■ ■ ■ ■ ■ ■ ■

Psalm 143:8

REST

WHAT HAPPENS
WHEN WE LIVE
GOD'S WAY? HE
BRINGS GIFTS INTO
OUR LIVES, MUCH
THE SAME WAY THAT
FRUIT APPEARS IN AN
ORCHARD—THINGS
LIKE AFFECTION
FOR OTHERS,
EXUBERANCE ABOUT
LIFE, SERENITY.

Galatians 5:22

$\mathcal{S}$urprise us with love at daybreak;
then we'll skip and dance all the day long....
Let your servants see what you're best at—
the ways you rule and bless your children.

REST

And let the loveliness of our Lord, our God,
rest on us,
confirming the work that we do.
Oh, yes. Affirm the work that we do!

■ ■ ■ ■ ■ ■ ■ ■ ■ ■ ■ ■ ■

Psalm 90:14,16-17

REST

I ask him that with both feet planted firmly on love, you'll be able to take in with all Christians the extravagant dimensions of Christ's love. Reach out and experience the breadth! Test its length! Plumb the depths! Rise to the heights! Live full lives, full in the fullness of God.

■ ■ ■ ■ ■ ■ ■ ■ ■ ■ ■ ■ ■ ■

Ephesians 3:17-18

REST

You never saw him, yet you love him. You still don't see him, yet you trust him…. Because you kept on believing, you'll get what you're looking forward to: total salvation.

■ ■ ■ ■ ■ ■ ■ ■ ■ ■ ■ ■ ■

1 Peter 1:8-9

What marvelous love the Father has extended to us! Just look at it—we're called children of God! That's who we really are.

■ ■ ■ ■ ■ ■ ■ ■ ■ ■ ■ ■ ■

1 John 3:1

REST

*I*t's impossible to please God apart from faith. And why? Because anyone who wants to approach God must believe both that he exists *and* that he cares enough to respond to those who seek him.

■ ■ ■ ■ ■ ■ ■ ■ ■ ■ ■ ■ ■ ■

Hebrews 11:6

REST

*R*elax, everything's going to be all right;
rest, everything's coming together;
open your hearts, love is on the way!

■ ■ ■ ■ ■ ■ ■ ■ ■ ■ ■ ■ ■ ■

Jude 1:2

R E S T

$\mathcal{G}$OD promises to love me all day,
sing songs all through the night!
My life is God's prayer.

∎ ∎ ∎ ∎ ∎ ∎ ∎ ∎ ∎ ∎ ∎ ∎ ∎ ∎

Psalm 42:8

REST

$\mathcal{I}$ pray to GOD—my life a prayer—
and wait for what he'll say and do....
With GOD's arrival comes love,
with GOD's arrival comes
generous redemption.

■■■■■■■■■■■■■■

Psalm 130:5,7

REST

SHOWERED
WITH
BLESSINGS

$\mathscr{G}$OD is gracious—it is he who makes
things right,
our most compassionate God.
GOD takes the side of the helpless;
when I was at the end of my rope, he saved me.

REST

I said to myself, "Relax and rest.
God has showered you with blessings."

■ ■ ■ ■ ■ ■ ■ ■ ■ ■ ■ ■ ■ ■

Psalm 116:5-7

REST

$\mathcal{Y}$our love, GOD, is my song, and I'll sing it!
I'm forever telling everyone how faithful you are.
I'll never quit telling the story of your love—
how you built the cosmos
and guaranteed everything in it.
Your love has always been our lives' foundation,
your fidelity has been the roof over our world....

REST

Search high and low, scan skies and land,
you'll find nothing and no one quite like GOD.
The holy angels are in awe before him;
he looms immense and august over
everyone around him.
GOD...who is like you,
powerful and faithful from every angle?

■ ■ ■ ■ ■ ■ ■ ■ ■ ■ ■ ■ ■ ■

Psalm 89:1-2,6-8

REST

$\mathcal{T}$hose who trust God's action in them
find that God's Spirit is in them—
living and breathing God!

■ ■ ■ ■ ■ ■ ■ ■ ■ ■ ■ ■ ■ ■

Romans 8:5

REST

$\mathcal{W}$e, your people, the ones you
love and care for,
will thank you over and over and over.
We'll tell everyone we meet
how wonderful you are, how
praiseworthy you are!

■ ■ ■ ■ ■ ■ ■ ■ ■ ■ ■ ■ ■ ■

Psalm 79:13

REST

*T*hose who trust in GOD
are like Zion Mountain:
Nothing can move it, a rock-solid mountain
you can always depend on.
Mountains encircle Jerusalem,
and GOD encircles his people—
always has and always will.

■ ■ ■ ■ ■ ■ ■ ■ ■ ■ ■ ■ ■ ■

Psalm 125:1-2

REST

You have bedded me down in
lush meadows,
you find me quiet pools to drink from.

■ ■ ■ ■ ■ ■ ■ ■ ■ ■ ■ ■ ■

Psalm 23:2

Give me space for healing, and mountain air.
Let me shout God's name with a praising song,
Let me tell his greatness in a prayer of thanks.

■ ■ ■ ■ ■ ■ ■ ■ ■ ■ ■ ■ ■

Psalm 69:29-30

REST

When I get really afraid
I come to you in trust.
I'm proud to praise God;
fearless now, I trust in God.

■ ■ ■ ■ ■ ■ ■ ■ ■ ■ ■ ■ ■ ■

Psalm 56:3-4

REST

REST

$\mathcal{B}$lessed are the people who know
the passwords of praise...
Delighted, they dance all day long; they know
who you are, what you do—
they can't keep it quiet!

REST

Your vibrant beauty has gotten inside us—
you've been so good to us!
We're walking on air!
All we are and have we owe to GOD.

■ ■ ■ ■ ■ ■ ■ ■ ■ ■ ■ ■ ■

Psalm 89:15-18

REST

Outlast the sun, outlive the moon—
age after age after age.
Be rainfall on cut grass,
earth-refreshing rain showers.

REST

Let righteousness burst into blossom
and peace abound until the moon fades
to nothing.
Rule from sea to sea,
from the River to the Rim.

■ ■ ■ ■ ■ ■ ■ ■ ■ ■ ■ ■ ■

Psalm 72:5-8

REST

*H*ow blessed all those in whom you live,
whose lives become roads you travel;
They wind through lonesome valleys,
come upon brooks,
discover cool springs and pools brimming
with rain!
God-traveled, these roads curve up
the mountain, and
at the last turn—Zion! God in full view!

■ ■ ■ ■ ■ ■ ■ ■ ■ ■ ■ ■ ■ ■

Psalm 84:5-7

REST

God, it seems you've been our home forever;
long before the mountains were born,
Long before you brought earth itself to birth,
from "once upon a time" to "kingdom come"—
you are God.

■ ■ ■ ■ ■ ■ ■ ■ ■ ■ ■ ■ ■ ■

Psalm 90:1-2

REST